heraldic Crests

A Pictorial Archive of 4,424 Designs for Artists and Craftspeople

JAMES FAIRBAIRN

DOVER PUBLICATIONS, INC.
NEW YORK

Copyright

Copyright © 1993 by Dover Publications, Inc.
All rights reserved under Pan American and International Copyright Conventions.

Published in Canada by General Publishing Company, Ltd., 30 Lesmill Road, Don Mills, Toronto, Ontario.
Published in the United Kingdom by Constable and Company, Ltd., 3 The Lanchesters, 162–164 Fulham Palace Road, London W6 9ER.

Bibliographical Note

This Dover edition, first published in 1993, contains all 314 plates originally published in *Fairbairn's Book of Crests of the Families of Great Britain and Ireland*, T. C. and E. C. Jack, London and Edinburgh, n.d. (fourth, revised and enlarged, edition of 1892 edition). See Publisher's Note for further information.

DOVER *Pictorial Archive* SERIES

This book belongs to the Dover Pictorial Archive Series. You may use the designs and illustrations for graphics and crafts applications, free and without special permission, provided that you include no more than ten in the same publication or project. (For permission for additional use, please write to Dover Publications, Inc., 31 East 2nd Street, Mineola, N.Y. 11501.)

However, republication or reproduction of any illustration by any other graphic service whether it be in a book or in any other design resource is strictly prohibited.

Library of Congress Cataloging-in-Publication Data

Fairbairn, James.
    [Fairbairn's book of crests of the families of Great Britain and Ireland. Selections]
    Heraldic crests : a pictorial archive of 4,424 designs for artists and crafts-people / James Fairbairn.
        p.   cm. — (Dover pictorial archive series)
    Originally published: Fairbairn's book of crests of the families of Great Britain and Ireland. 4th ed., rev. and enl. London : T.C. & E.C. Jack, 1912. Vol. 2.
    ISBN 0-486-27713-5
    1. Heraldry—Great Britain.   2. Heraldry—Ireland.   3. Crests—Great Britain.   4. Crests—Ireland.   I. Title.   II. Series.
CR57.G7F25   1993
929.6'0941—dc20   93-15692
                                                                                                            CIP

Manufactured in the United States of America
Dover Publications, Inc., 31 East 2nd Street, Mineola, N.Y. 11501

PUBLISHER'S NOTE

Fairbairn's Book of Crests was first published in 1859. It was originally compiled by the Scotsman James Fairbairn and later revised by Lawrence Butters, Seal Engraver in Ordinary to Her Majesty [Victoria Regina] for Scotland. Fairbairn's collection of armorial bearings then went through a number of editions into which literally thousands of bogus coats-of-arms or crests managed to creep. The editor of the 1892 edition, and a giant in the science and art of heraldry, the Englishman A. C. Fox-Davies, detected a vast quantity of the unlicensed blazons and determined that they had been added to the original collection over the years owing to its use by jewelers and seal engravers. Fox-Davies thoroughly overhauled and revised Fairbairn's Book of Crests under the direction of the publisher T. C. and E. C. Jack of London and Edinburgh. He discarded these unauthorized crests and created the modern collection before us today.

In his "Editor's Preface to Revised Edition,"* Fox-Davies explained that "the whole of the Illustrations of the last Edition have been carefully examined. Some have been altered and some rejected, and over One Thousand New Crests have been added to those previously appearing. It has been one great anxiety that the Illustrations, however slightly they might differ, should not be quoted as correct unless they actually were so. . . ."

In using the word "correct," Fox-Davies took pains to make it clear that he was "not referring to mediæval or antique styles of draughtsmanship," but to the way in which a blazon is painted on a royal grant. He did acknowledge, however, that his selection of one blazon over another probably resulted from the "garrulous minuteness" of his own English school of arms versus the far freer Scottish practice. He made no claim that his selections were beyond reproach, but the labor of love left to us by the foremost modern authority on the subject speaks for itself.

While clearly stating that the selection of a crest is not a matter of choice, and railing against the "heraldic stationer who, for a trifling fee, professes, on receipt of 'name and county,' to find armorial bearings for any applicant," Fox-Davies took pains to say that he could not claim authority on questions regarding the right of any person to a particular crest. Thanks to the growing contemporary interest in the art of heraldry, and a lapse in the laws strictly regulating such, artists and designers today will find that the reproductions of nineteenth-century engravings in the present volume are highly desirable for their own new projects. The 4,424 exquisite engravings that make up this book rank among the finest sources of illustration for many design purposes.

---

*Note: All quotations are from A. C. Fox-Davies, ed., *Fairbairn's Book of Crests of the Families of Great Britain and Ireland*, rev. ed. (London and Edinburgh: T. C. and E. C. Jack, 1892), pp. i–iv.

PLATE 1

PLATE 2

PLATE 3

PLATE 4

PLATE 5

1

2

3

4

5

6

7

8

9

10

11

12

13

14

15

PLATE 6

PLATE 7

PLATE 8

PLATE 9

1

2

3

4

5

6

7

8

9

10

11

12

13

14

15

PLATE 10

PLATE II

PLATE 12

PLATE 13

PLATE 14

PLATE 15

PLATE 16

PLATE 17

PLATE 18

PLATE 19

1

2

3

4

5

6

7

8

9

10

11

12

PLATE 20

1

2

3

4

5

6

7

8

9

10

11

12

PLATE 21

1

2

3

4

5

6

7

8

9

10

11

12

PLATE 22

PLATE 23

PLATE 24

PLATE 25

PLATE 26

PLATE 27

PLATE 28

PLATE 29

PLATE 30

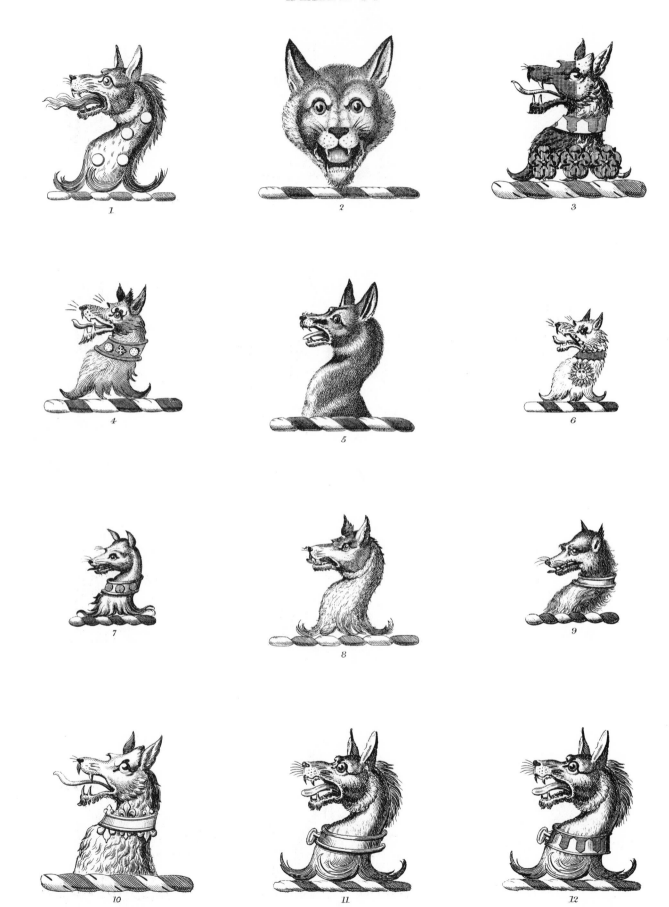

PLATE 31

PLATE 32

1

2

3

4

5

6

7

8

9

10

11

12

PLATE 33

1

2

3

4

5

6

7

8

9

10

11

12

PLATE 34

1

2

3

4

5

6

7

8

9

10

11

12

13

14

PLATE 35

1

2

3

4

5

6

7

8

9

10

11

12

PLATE 36

PLATE 37

PLATE 38

PLATE 39

PLATE 40

1

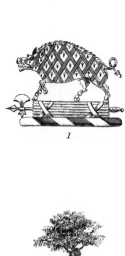

2

3

4

5

6

7

8

9

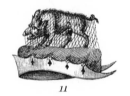

10

11

12

13

14

PLATE 41

PLATE 42

PLATE 43

1

2

3

4

5

6

7

8

9

10

11

12

PLATE 44

1

2

3

4

5

6

7

8

9

10

11

12

PLATE 45

PLATE 46

1

2

3

4

5

6

7

8

9

10

11

12

PLATE 47

1

2

3

4

4

5

6

7

8

9

10

11

12

PLATE 48

PLATE 49

PLATE 50

PLATE 51

PLATE 52

PLATE 53

PLATE 54

1

2

3

4

5

6

7

8

9

10

11

12

13

14

PLATE 55

PLATE 56

PLATE 57

PLATE 58

1

2

3

4

5

6

7

5

9

10

8

11

12

13

14

PLATE 59

1

2

3

4

5

6

7

8

9

10

11

12

13

14

PLATE 60

PLATE 61

PLATE 62

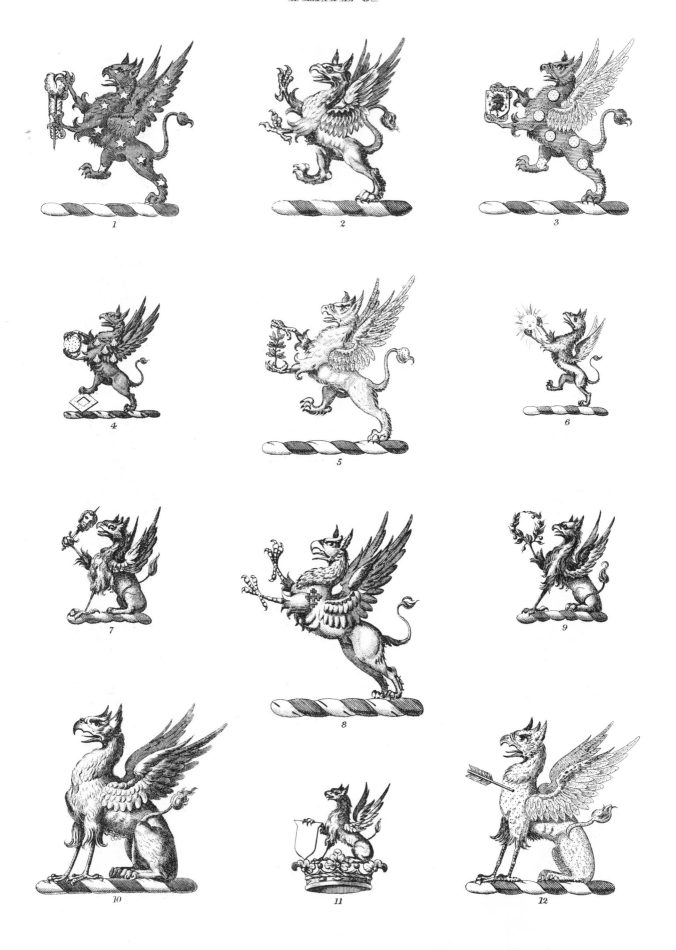

1

2

3

4

5

6

7

8

9

10

11

12

PLATE 63

PLATE 64

PLATE 65

1

2

3

4

5

6

7

8

9

10

11

12

13

14

PLATE 66

PLATE 67

PLATE 68

PLATE 69

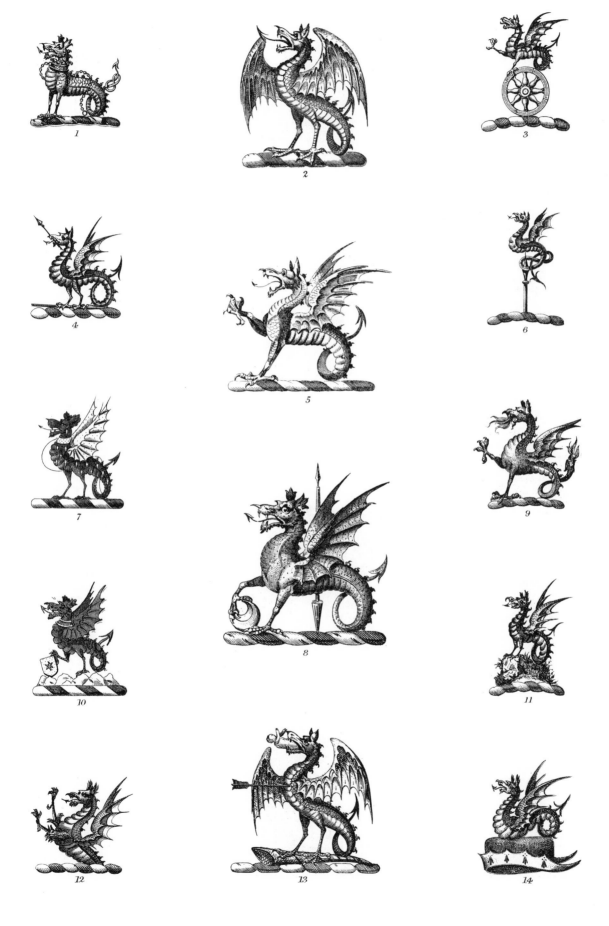

PLATE 70

PLATE 71

PLATE 72

PLATE 73

PLATE 74

PLATE 75

PLATE 76

PLATE 77

PLATE 78

PLATE 79

PLATE 80

PLATE 81

PLATE 82

PLATE 83

PLATE 84

1

2

3

4

5

6

7

8

9

10

11

12

13

14

15

PLATE 85

PLATE 86

PLATE 87

PLATE 88

PLATE 89

PLATE 90

PLATE 91

PLATE 92

PLATE 93

PLATE 94

PLATE 95

1

2

3

4

5

6

7

8

9

10

11

12

PLATE 96

1

2

3

4

5

6

7

8

9

10

11

12

PLATE 97

PLATE 98

PLATE 99

PLATE 100

PLATE 101

PLATE 102

1

2

3

4

5

6

7

8

9

10

11

12

PLATE 103

PLATE 104

PLATE 105

PLATE 106

PLATE 107

PLATE 108

1

2

3

4

5

6

7

8

9

10

11

12

PLATE 109

PLATE 110

PLATE III

PLATE 112

1

2

3

4

5

6

7

8

9

10

11

12

13

PLATE 113

PLATE 114

PLATE 115

PLATE 116

PLATE 117

PLATE 118

PLATE 119

PLATE 120

1

2

3

4

5

6

7

8

9

10

11

12

13

14

PLATE 121

PLATE 122

PLATE 123

PLATE 124

PLATE 125

1

2

3

4

5

6

7

8

9

10

11

12

PLATE 126

PLATE 127

PLATE 128

PLATE 129

PLATE 130

PLATE 131

PLATE 132

PLATE 133

1

2

3

4

5

6

7

8

9

10

11

12

PLATE 134

PLATE 135

PLATE 136

PLATE 137

1

2

3

4

5

6

7

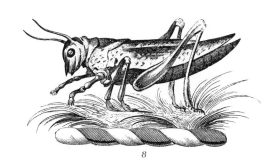

8

9

10

11

12

PLATE 138

1

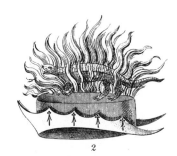

2

3

4

5

6

7

8

9

10

11

12

PLATE 139

1

2

3

4

5

6

7

8

9

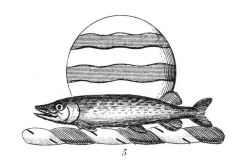

10

11

12

13

14

PLATE 140

1

2

3

4

5

6

7

8

9

10

11

12

PLATE 141

1

2

3

4

5

6

7

8

9

10

11

12

13

14

PLATE 142

1

2

3

4

5

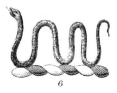

6

7

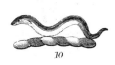

8

9

10

11

12

13

14

PLATE 143

PLATE 144

PLATE 145

PLATE 146

PLATE 147

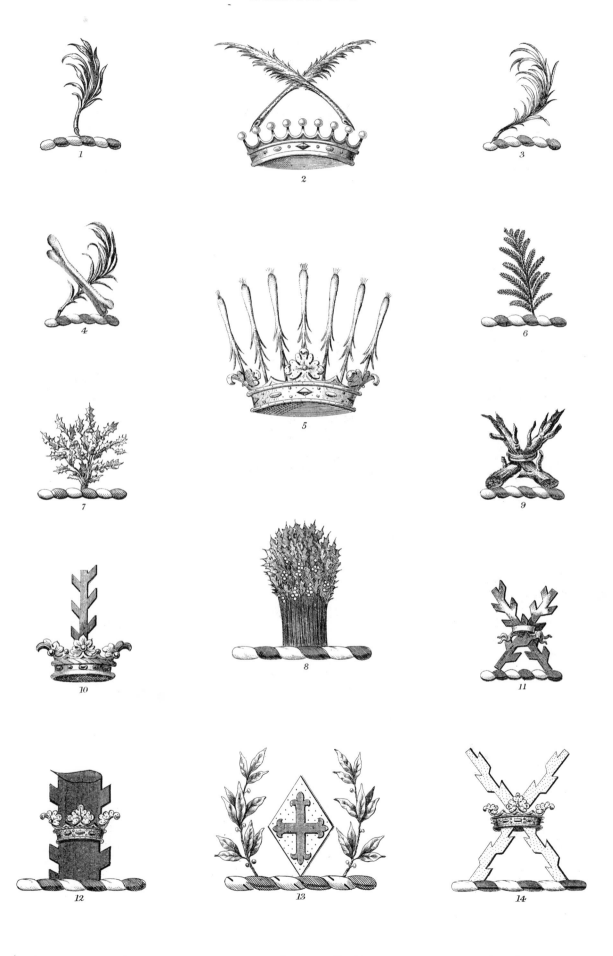

PLATE 148

1

2

3

4

5

6

7

8

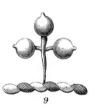

9

10

11

12

PLATE 149

PLATE 150

1

2

3

4

5

6

7

8

9

10

11

12

PLATE 151

PLATE 152

PLATE 153

PLATE 154

PLATE 155

1

2

3

4

5

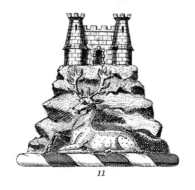

6

7

8

9

10

11

12

PLATE 156

PLATE 157

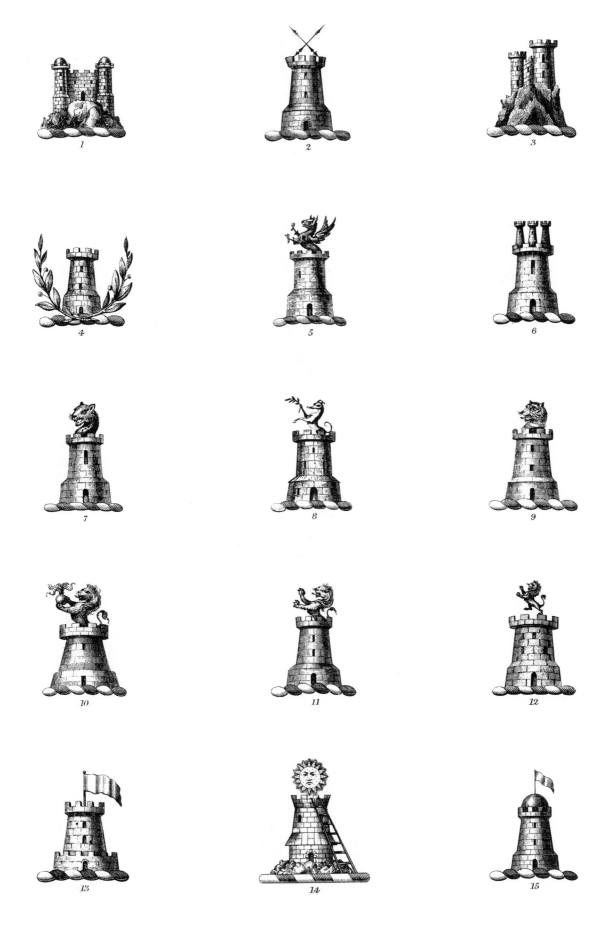

PLATE 158

1

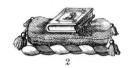

2

3

4

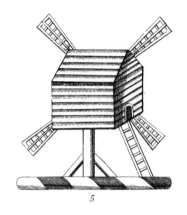

5

6

7

8

9

10

11

12

13

14

PLATE 159

1

2

3

4

5

6

7

8

9

10

11

12

13

14

15

PLATE 160

PLATE 161

1

2

3

4

5

6

7

8

9

10

11

12

PLATE 162

PLATE 163

PLATE 164

1

2

3

4

5

6

7

8

9

10

11

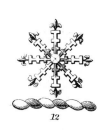

12

13

14

PLATE 165

PLATE 166

PLATE 167

1

2

3

4

5

6

7

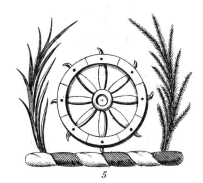

8

9

10

11

12

13

14

PLATE 168

PLATE 169

1

2

3

4

5

6

7

8

9

10

11

12

PLATE 170

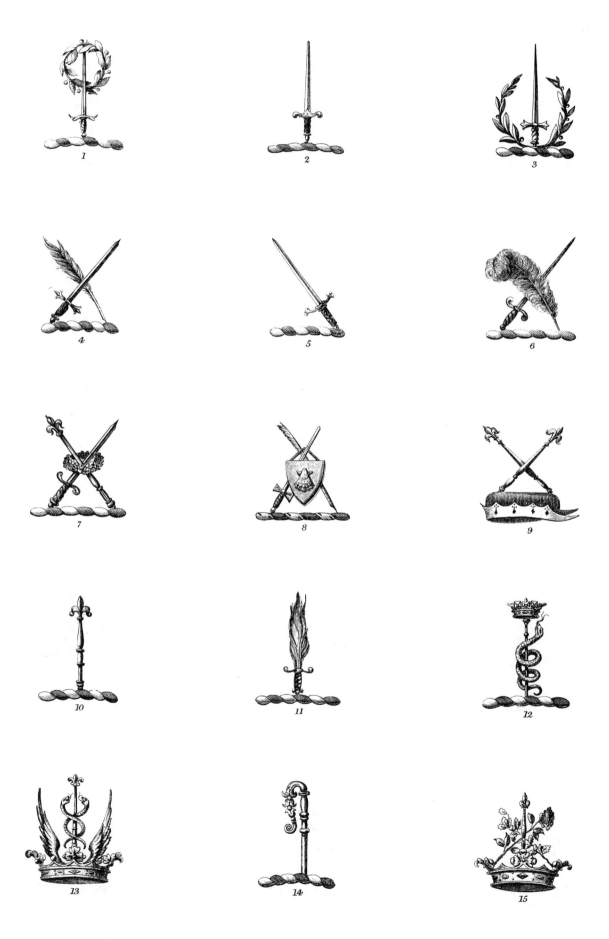

PLATE 171

PLATE 172

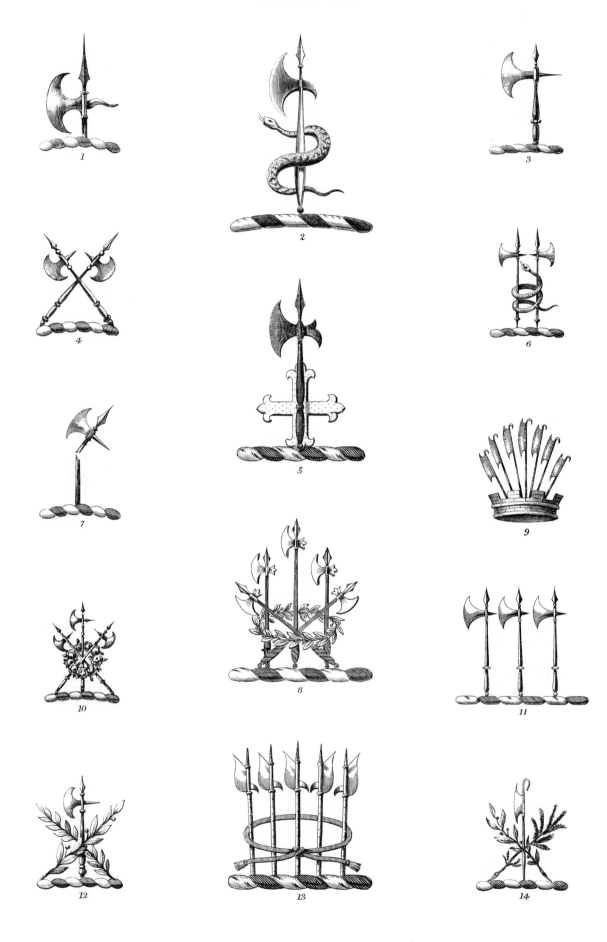

PLATE 173

PLATE 174

1

2

3

4

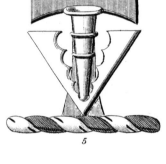

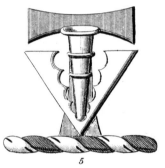

5

6

7

8

9

10

11

12

13

14

PLATE 175

PLATE 176

PLATE 177

PLATE 178

1

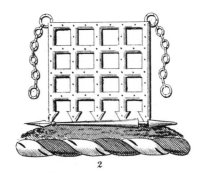

2

3

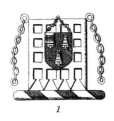

4

5

6

7

8

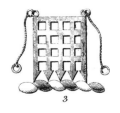

9

10

11

12

PLATE 179

1

2

3

4

5

6

7

8

9

10

11

12

PLATE 180

PLATE 181

PLATE 182

PLATE 183

PLATE 184

PLATE 185

1

2

3

4

5

6

7

8

9

10

11

12

PLATE 186

PLATE 187

PLATE 188

PLATE 189

PLATE 190

PLATE 191

PLATE 192

PLATE 193

PLATE 194

PLATE 195

PLATE 196

PLATE 197

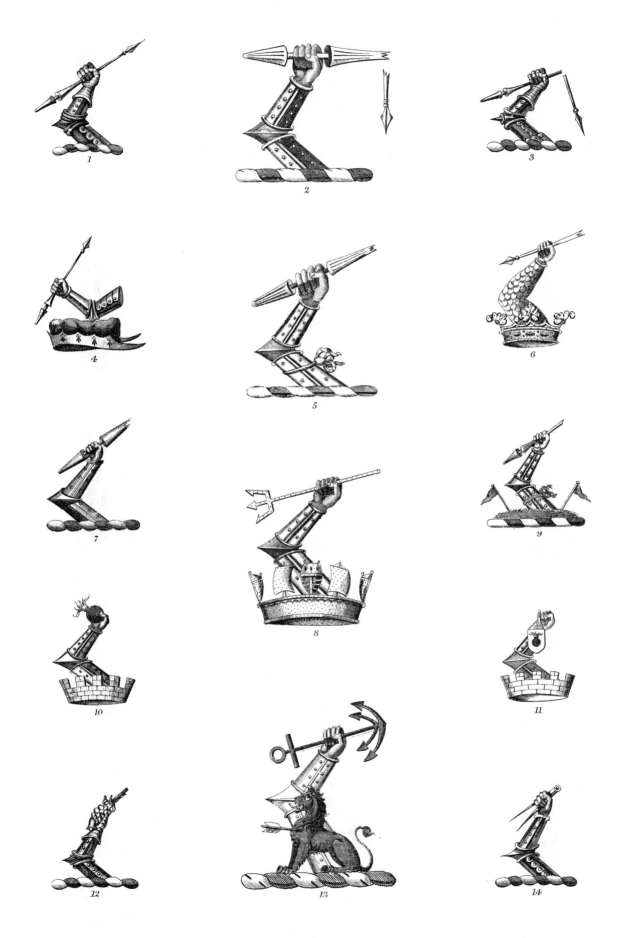

PLATE 198

PLATE 199

PLATE 200

1

2

3

4

5

6

7

8

9

10

11

12

PLATE 201

PLATE 202

PLATE 203

PLATE 204

PLATE 205

PLATE 206

PLATE 207

PLATE 208

PLATE 209

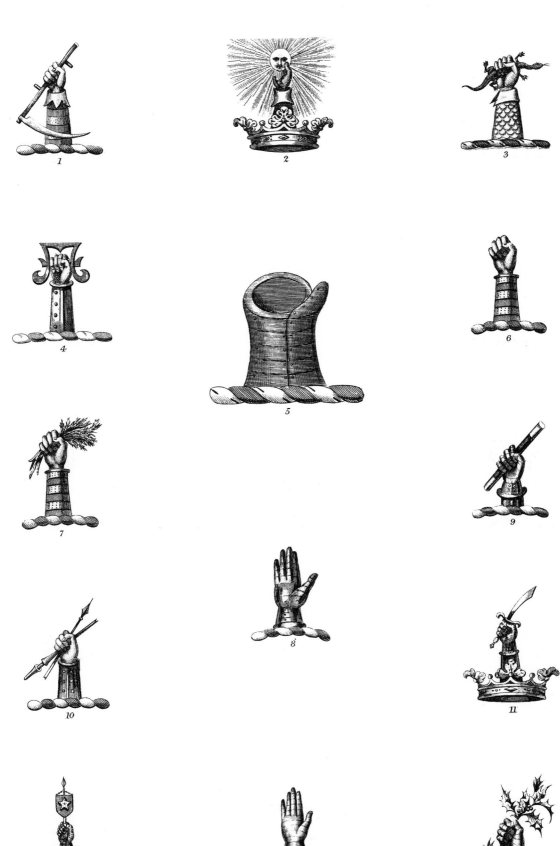

PLATE 210

PLATE 211

PLATE 212

PLATE 213

PLATE 214

PLATE 215

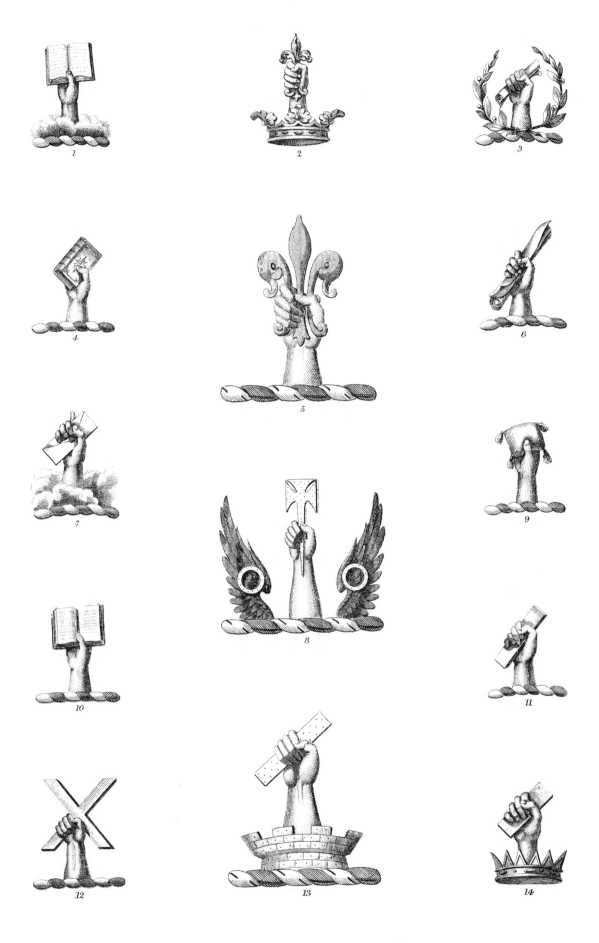

PLATE 216

PLATE 217

PLATE 218

PLATE 219

PLATE 220

1

2

3

4

5

6

7

8

9

10

11

12

PLATE 221

PLATE 222

PLATE 223

1

2

3

4

5

6

7

8

9

10

11

12

PLATE 224

PLATE 225

PLATE 226

PLATE 227

PLATE 228

PLATE 229

1

2

3

4

5

6

7

8

9

10

11

12

PLATE 230

PLATE 231

1

2

3

4

5

6

7

8

9

10

11

12

13

14

15

16

17

18

19

20

21

PLATE 232

PLATE 233

1

2

3

4

5

6

7

8

9

10

11

12

13

14

15

16

PLATE 234

PLATE 235

PLATE 236

1

2

3

4

5

6

7

8

9

10

II

12

PLATE 237

PLATE 238

PLATE 239

1

2

3

4

5

6

7

8

9

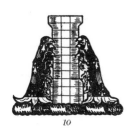

10

11

12

PLATE 240

PLATE 241

1

2

3

4

5

6

7

8

9

10

11

12

13

14

15

16

PLATE 242

1

2

3

4

5

6

7

8

9

PLATE 243

1

2

3

4

5

6

7

8

9

10

11

12

13

14

15

16

17

18

19

20

PLATE 244

1

2

3

4

5

6

7

8

9

10

11

12

13

14

15

16

17

18

19

20

PLATE 245

1

2

3

4

5

6

7

8

9

10

11

12

PLATE 246

PLATE 247

PLATE 248

1

2

3

4

5

6

7

8

9

PLATE 249

PLATE 250

PLATE 251

1

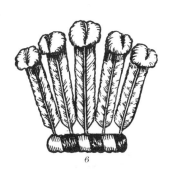

2

3

4

5

6

7

8

9

10

11

12

PLATE 252

PLATE 253

1

2

3

4

5

6

7

8

9

10

11

12

13

14

15

16

17

18

19

20

21

22

23

24

PLATE 254

PLATE 255

PLATE 256

PLATE 257

PLATE 258

PLATE 259

PLATE 260

PLATE 261

PLATE 262

PLATE 263

PLATE 264

1

2

3

4

5

6

7

8

9

10

11

12

13

14

15

16

PLATE 265

1

2

3

4

5

6

7

8

9

10

11

12

13

14

15

16

PLATE 266

1

2

3

4

5

6

7

8

9

10

11

12

13

14

15

16

PLATE 267

1

2

3

4

5

6

7

8

9

10

11

12

13

14

15

16

PLATE 268

1

2

3

4

5

6

7

8

9

10

11

12

13

14

15

16

PLATE 269

1

2

3

4

5

6

7

8

9

10

11

12

13

14

15

16

17

18

19

20

PLATE 270

SOIES CONTENT

2

1

3

VIVE UT VIVAS

4

VIRTUTE·GLORIA·MERCES

5

FAC·ET·SPERA

6

DEO NON FORTUNA

7

IN UTROQUE FIDELI

8

9

10

11

12

PLATE 271

1

2 REVIRESGAM

3

4

5

6

7

8

9

10

11

12

13

14

15

16

17

18

19

20

21 DULCIUS EX ASPERIS

PLATE 272

PLATE 273

1

2

3

4

5

6

7

8

9

10

11

12

13

14

15

PLATE 274

PLATE 275

PLATE 276

PLATE 277

1

2

3

4

5

6

7

8

9

10

11

12

13

14

15

PLATE 278

PLATE 279

1

2

3

4

5

6

7

8

9

10

11

12

13

14

15

PLATE 280

PLATE 281

1

2

3

4

5

6

7

8

9

10

11

12

13

14

15

PLATE 282

1

2

3

4

5

6

7

8

9

10

11

12

13

14

15

PLATE 283

PLATE 284

1

2

3

4

5

6

7

8

9

10

11

12

13

14

15

PLATE 285

1

2

3

4

5

6

7

8

9

10

11

12

13

14

15

PLATE 286

PLATE 287

PLATE 288

PLATE 289

1   2   3

4   5   6

7   8   9

10   11   12

13   14   15

PLATE 290

PLATE 291

PLATE 292

1

2

3

4

5

6

7

8

9

10

11

12

13

14

15

PLATE 293

PLATE 294

PLATE 295

PLATE 296

PLATE 297

PLATE 298

PLATE 299

PLATE 300

PLATE 301

1

2

3

4

5

6

7

8

9

10

11

12

13

14

15

PLATE 302

PLATE 303

PLATE 304

PLATE 305

PLATE 306

PLATE 307

PLATE 308

PLATE 309

PLATE 310

1

2

3

4

5

6

7

8

9

10

11

12

13

14

15

PLATE 311

PLATE 312

PLATE 313

PLATE 314

1

2

3

4

5

6

7

8

9